Ronald J. Ryan, CFA
CEO, Ryan ALM, Inc.
Palm Beach Gardens, Florida

The Evolution of Asset/Liability Management

RESEARCH FOUNDATION
OF CFA INSTITUTE

Statement of Purpose

The Research Foundation of CFA Institute is a not-for-profit organization established to promote the development and dissemination of relevant research for investment practitioners worldwide.

ISBN 978-1-934667-62-0

24 September 2013

The Evolution of Asset/Liability Management

Ronald J. Ryan, CFA
CEO, Ryan ALM, Inc.
Palm Beach Gardens, Florida

This review tracks the development of asset/liability management from its roots in liability management outsourcing to its most recent interpretation as a broad liability-driven investing strategy.

What Is Asset/Liability Management?

The objective of most institutions in the United States with assets to invest is to fund some sort of liability, as is the case with banks, insurance companies, pension funds, and so forth. As a result, asset/liability management should be the investment focus and the basis for selecting the core portfolio.

Alone among major types of institutions, insurance companies have maintained this focus because it is required by the regulations under which they operate. The IAIS Standard No. 13 (2006), which is the basis for insurance company regulation in the United States, defines asset/liability management (ALM) as the practice of managing a business so that decisions and actions taken with respect to assets and liabilities are coordinated.[1] Oracle Financial Services (2008), in its white paper "Asset Liability Management: An Overview," defines ALM for banks as a mechanism to address the risk faced by a bank because of a mismatch between assets and liabilities resulting from either differences in liquidity or changes in interest rates. Brick (2012), in his paper "Asset-Liability Management: Theory, Practice, and the Role of Judgment," provides an in-depth analysis of the ALM practices of banks and defines ALM as the process that deals with interest rate risk management.

Indeed, as banks and insurance companies have practiced it, ALM is the management of assets so that their interest rate risk matches, or is as similar as possible to, that of the liabilities. Exley, Mehta, and Smith (1997) conclude in their paper "The Financial Theory of Defined Benefit Pension Schemes" that financial theory offers no good reason why ALM as practiced by pensions should differ from ALM by banks. They emphasize that the time has come to stop treating pensions as anything special. Pension liabilities are the

[1]IAIS is the International Association of Insurance Supervisors. See http://www.iaisweb.com.

same as any other liability. In a special LDI (liability-driven investing) issue of *aiCIO Magazine*, McDaniel (2011) provides a well-documented history of LDI theory in his column "LDI's Founding Document," concluding that pension liabilities should be treated in the same way as bank and insurance liabilities, giving each a proper ALM focus.

The focus of this literature review will be the evolution of ALM for pensions. Pensions have no regulations requiring asset/liability management or the matching of asset risk to liability risk. This lack of regulation may be the most important cause of the ballooning pension deficits of the last 13 years.

The history of formal ALM (sometimes referred to as liability-driven investing, or LDI) is littered with false starts. The most prolific author on ALM for pensions is Martin Leibowitz, who has produced numerous papers and books over the last 40 years. Fifty-seven of his articles were collected and edited by Frank Fabozzi in a book simply titled *Investing* (Leibowitz 1992), which contains a wealth of ALM analysis, theories, and strategies.

Prehistory: Insurance Company Management of Pension Funds

In the decades before pension plan sponsors began to manage pension assets as quasi-independent investment organizations, it was typical for sponsors to simply pay an insurance company to assume the liabilities of the pension plan. The insurance company was then responsible for investing the assets while complying with then-current insurance regulations. Naturally, the insurance companies invested most of these assets in fixed-income securities, often matching the cash flows from the assets to the cash required to be paid to the pension beneficiaries. This historical period from roughly 1875 (when the first U.S. corporate pension plan, that of American Express, was established) to the 1960s is described in "Evolution of Employer-Provided Defined Benefit Plans" (Seburn 1991).

In the Beginning: Dedication

Dedication was the earliest form of ALM practiced by pension plans as quasi-independent investment organizations. It was in vogue during the historically high-interest-rate environment of the late 1970s and early 1980s. Leibowitz was the first to refer to cash flow matching as "dedication" because it required matching a stream of cash inflows (assets) to a stream of cash outflows (liabilities); each cash inflow was "dedicated" to paying a particular outflow. His work was initially published by Salomon Brothers, where he was managing director, and then (1986a, 1986b) as a series in the *Financial Analysts Journal* under the titles "The Dedicated Bond Portfolio in Pension Funds." Many authors have written about the pros and cons of dedication. Perhaps the most complete set of writings is offered by Fabozzi in *The Handbook of Fixed Income Securities* (see Fabozzi 2005a, 2005b).

The dedication model assumed a 100% bond portfolio held to maturity. The quest was to find the least expensive collection of bonds that provided the needed cash flows over the time horizon of the program. Dedication had several distinct advantages:

1. Predictable cash flows (when the bonds are held to maturity),
2. Reduction of risk (market, reinvestment, inflation, default, and liquidity risks),
3. Specificity (asset cash flows must match liability cash flows),
4. Simple asset allocation (100% bonds), and
5. Passive management (more certain returns with lower fees).

Dedication also had several disadvantages, which in time may have led to its undoing as a core strategy for pension plans:

1. Difficulty of construction (became the domain of broker/dealers and eliminated many asset managers and competitors),
2. Complicated mathematical models (hard to understand for many clients),
3. Requirement for accurate projected liability benefit payments (cash flows), which challenged actuaries,
4. Need to match future values, not present values (created potential volatility of funded ratio, or asset/liability ratio, if assets did not behave in sync with liabilities),
5. Reduction or even elimination of the role of active bond managers and pension consultants for asset allocation, and
6. Highly interest-rate-sensitive cost (inversely correlated with interest rates).

Immunization Replaces Dedication as an ALM Strategy

In the 1980s, dedication gave way to immunization, which focuses on matching the interest rate movement of liabilities in present value dollars. The idea is to minimize the volatility of the surplus (the dollar value of assets minus liabilities) by having an asset duration equal to the liability duration. Duration is the present-value-weighted average time to receipt of the cash flows from a security or portfolio. Macaulay (1938), in his book titled *Some Theoretical Problems Suggested by the Movement of Interest Rates, Bond Yields and*

Stock Prices in the United States since 1856,[2] is credited with introducing the term "duration" and defining it as I have above. In 1942, Koopmans's paper "The Risk of Interest Fluctuations in Life Insurance Companies" pointed out that if the duration of the bonds held in a portfolio were matched to the duration of the liabilities those bonds would fund, the effects of interest rate changes could be mitigated or nullified completely (i.e., the portfolio would be immunized). In 1945, Samuelson's paper "The Effect of Interest Rate Increases on the Banking System" formulated essentially the same concept, calling it the "weighted average time period." None of these scholars cited the others' work, suggesting that each developed the concept independently.

The effort to define ALM strategies that would neutralize or match interest rate sensitivity of assets versus liabilities, largely conducted by academics, culminated in a 1952 paper titled "Review of the Principles of Life-Office Valuations" by a nonacademic actuary, F.M. Redington, who worked for a British insurance company. He is credited with introducing the term "immunization" to signify the investment of assets in such a way that the existing business is immune to a general change in the interest rate. This body of work was largely ignored until 1971, when Fisher and Weil reintroduced immunization to the academic community in the journal article "Coping with the Risk of Interest-Rate Fluctuations: Returns to Bondholders from Naïve and Optimal Strategies." Shortly thereafter, in 1972, Vanderhoof presented "The Effects of Interest Rate Assumption and the Maturity Structure of the Assets of a Life Insurance Company" to the American actuarial community.

Academic papers on immunization, duration, and dedication began to appear in increasing numbers. As interest rates rose in a long secular trend, the financial industry began to pay attention. Realizing that the high interest rates would allow them to lock in unprecedented rates of return, defined benefit pension fund managers embraced the concepts of dedication and then immunization. Wall Street broker/dealers, especially Salomon Brothers, with Leibowitz as its intellectual leader, provided the complicated software models needed to execute dedication and immunization effectively. Many papers promoting and critiquing immunization strategies were written by quantitative scholars during this time. Among them are Keintz and Stickney's (1980) "Immunization of Pension Funds and Sensitivity to Actuarial Assumptions," Fong and Vasicek's (1984) "A Risk Minimizing Strategy for Portfolio Immunization," Leibowitz's (1986b) "The Dedicated Bond Portfolio in Pension Funds—Part II: Immunization, Horizon Matching and Contingent Procedures," Maloney and Yawitz's (1986) "Interest Rate Risk, Immunization and Duration," Williams's

[2]This title is often shortened to *The Movement of Interest Rates, Bond Yields and Stock Prices in the United States since 1856*.

(1992) "Managing Asset/Liability Portfolios—An Overview," and Fooladi's (2000) "Risk Management with Duration Analysis."

Times were good for broker/dealers who could execute very large dedication and immunization portfolios. Perhaps the largest bond trades ever recorded were those done for dedication and immunization as single, very large orders. However, things were not so good for many active bond managers and pension consultants, who saw their clients' demand for active bond managers and asset allocation models dwindling.

As interest rates began to fall in early 1982, call risk surfaced as a serious impediment to immunization and dedication models, especially for those who ventured into mortgage-backed securities. This call (or prepayment) risk would alter cash flows and maturity structures, with resulting damage to the integrity of immunization and dedication models that depended on the certainty of these cash flows and maturity dates. Thompson, in his 1981 comments on Keintz and Stickney's (1980) paper, warned that immunization programs were vulnerable to these risks.

As a solution to the problems with immunization, Leibowitz and Weinberger (1982) offered a new financial discipline they called "contingent immunization." They defined contingent immunization as what we would now call a form of portfolio insurance. The portfolio remains in an active management mode, attempting to beat the market or a market benchmark, as long as the portfolio's asset value places it above some prespecified minimum value relative to liabilities. The portfolio enters an immunization mode only when it falls below that value—that is, when absolutely necessary to ensure a promised minimum return. Contingent immunization seemed to offer the best of both worlds—the pursuit of maximum returns through active management and the limitation of downside risk through immunization.

Because immunization strategies focus on matching the present values of assets and liabilities, it is important to determine what discount rates to use to calculate the present value of liabilities. Choie (1992), in "Caveats in Immunization of Pension Liabilities," stated that the first issue in immunization is establishing the appropriate discount rates to use to compute the present value and the duration of a liability schedule. He recommended using a yield curve of spreads off the Treasury yield curve on a certain credit rating (AA corporates) as the discount rates.

Accounting Rules Redirect Pension Asset Management

When the Financial Accounting Standards Board (FASB) issued its Statement of Financial Accounting Standards No. 87 in 1985 (effective December 1986), it marked both a good and bad moment in the evolution of asset/liability management. First, it clarified that the discount rate methodology used for liabilities should be based on a high-quality bond yield curve that settles the liabilities. This standard would help those designing immunization strategies to understand how to match the present value of liabilities. However, for pension expense purposes, the new statement allowed corporations to use the return on assets (ROA) assumption as follows: If the dollar growth in pension assets based on the ROA rate exceeded the pension expense amount, then pension expense would be negative—that is, it would become pension *income*, which would directly enhance earnings. Because corporations tend to maximize earnings per share (EPS) rather than minimize the risk of not being able to pay liabilities, the ROA became the hurdle rate or rate-of-return objective for pension assets.

When interest rates went below the ROA assumption rate (around 8%) in the late 1980s, dedication and immunization strategies fell out of vogue because they locked in a return that would not be sufficient to neutralize or overcome pension expense, resulting in a drain on, or a charge against, EPS. As a consequence, dedication and immunization were largely replaced by surplus optimization strategies that aimed for the growth of pension assets to outpace liability growth, thereby creating a pension surplus that would reduce or even eliminate contribution costs. Contribution costs were a function of the funded ratio (the present value of assets expressed as a percentage of the present value of liabilities). Any deficit or underfunding (a funded ratio less than 100%) was to be erased through contributions planned out over time so that the pension plan would be fully funded over a designated time horizon. The Treasury supplied the discount rates used to calculate the present value of liabilities, and these rates were based on the 30-year Treasury yield. Assets were valued as a moving average of market values (usually a five-year average).

The late 1980s and the decade of the 1990s were good times for pensions. With the switch to a surplus optimization strategy, asset allocation models now favored equities over bonds because the ROA was now the "bogey," or investment return benchmark. This asset allocation decision worked out well during this period; equities enjoyed several good years of double-digit returns, resulting in pension surpluses that enhanced EPS (returns above the ROA were an "actuarial gain" line item that increased EPS) and reduced or eliminated contribution costs. During this period, ALM became a hard sell, given the level of interest rates, the historical return track record of equities, and the resulting financial statement benefits of an ROA hurdle rate. This focus on an absolute return (ROA) rather than on return relative to liability growth would soon haunt the pension industry and prove fatal to some (by driving sponsors into bankruptcy).

The equity bear market that hit in 2000–2002 became a pension tsunami for several reasons. The correction was quite deep, amounting to a 49% fall in the S&P 500 Index, with the result that pension asset growth underperformed liability growth by as much as 75% on a cumulative basis over those three years. This event led to spiraling contribution costs because of crashing funded ratios, an EPS drain from the pension assets underperforming the ROA (actuarial loss), and in some cases, insolvency of the sponsor, with several companies (notably airlines) filing for bankruptcy because pensions tend to be the largest liability of many firms.

The Society of Actuaries (SOA) had been concerned that such an asset/liability disparity would occur as a result of accounting rules, and it issued a research paper draft (2004) titled "Principles Underlying Asset Liability Management," which warned that accounting measures distort economic reality and produce reports that are inconsistent with economic results. It further stated that entities that focus on economic value tend to achieve their financial objectives more consistently in the long run. In other words, the SOA promoted ALM on an economic (i.e., market value) basis, rather than on an accounting basis, as the proper asset management style.

At roughly that time, however, corporations were begging for relief from spiking pension contribution costs. Congress responded with the Pension Protection Act (PPA) of 2006. A number of pension experts provided testimony during the several-years-long process of writing the PPA. In my "Testimony before the ERISA Advisory Council on Employee Welfare and Pension Benefit Plans" (Ryan 2003), I recommended that liabilities should be priced at the market as a yield curve. I further proposed that a rule should be created and enforced that reads, "If you cannot buy it, you cannot use it as a discount rate!"

In the end, PPA legislation relaxed the contribution costs calculation by offering two ways to discount liabilities: (1) a 24-month moving average of a three-segment yield curve and (2) the current spot-rate yield curve. In both options, the yield curve was based on high-quality corporate bonds rather than Treasury bonds. In effect, the PPA raised discount rates and lowered the apparent present value of liabilities, thereby enhancing the apparent funded ratio and lowering contribution requirements.

The FASB was also concerned that existing standards did not communicate the funded status on balance sheets, so in 2006 it issued Statement of Accounting Standards No. 158: *Employers' Accounting for Defined Benefit Pension and Other Postretirement Plans* (effective 2007). This communication, usually referred to as FAS 158, clarified that the discount rates used should correspond to the current market value of a portfolio of high-quality zero-coupon bonds whose maturity dates and amounts match the expected future benefit payments. This accounting standard also introduced Other Post-Employment Benefits (OPEB) liabilities onto the balance sheet, revealing that they are one of the largest liabilities facing U.S. institutions.

ALM Strategies Reborn as LDI

After the equity correction of 2000–2003, the stage was set for institutions to return to the basic practice of asset/liability management, because failure to do so had resulted in deteriorating funded ratios, large actuarial losses, and spiking contribution costs. This time, however, ALM was more frequently referred to as liability-driven investing (LDI) to suggest a new, enhanced approach. Ehrentreich (2009), in his paper "The Asset Return–Funding Cost Paradox: The Case for LDI," succinctly stated that under current pension regulations, there is no place for equities in defined benefit plans. Moreover, there is no incentive to overfund a pension plan. Equity-based investment strategies sooner or later lead to large funding shortfalls, and the inability of most plan sponsors to close them immediately makes them persistent.

But because of the ongoing secular trend toward lower rates and the fact that the expected return on assets continued to be used to calculate pension expense, corporations continued to pursue an asset allocation away from bonds but with less equity concentration. This trend opened the asset allocation door to many new asset classes and strategies, including hedge funds and other alternative investments, 130–30 (that is, 130% long and 30% short) portfolios, and new LDI strategies.

Fabozzi and I have written prolifically on ALM strategies and considerations. Fabozzi's books are a mainstay for any ALM practitioner. His *Bond Portfolio Management* (especially the chapter "Managing Funds Against Liabilities"), published in 2001, and *The Handbook of Fixed Income Securities* (especially the chapter "Bond Immunization: An Asset/Liability Optimization Strategy"), published in 2005, have become required reading.

Fabozzi and I teamed up in 2005 to produce the article "Reforming Pension Reform," proposing a solution to the growing pension crisis. Our solution starts with pricing liabilities at the market (economic value) and then building a custom liability index as the proper benchmark for pensions (or any liability-driven objective), because liabilities are unique to each pension plan. We later followed this article with "Liability Index Fund: The Liability Beta Portfolio" (2011), in which we argued that a liability index fund should be the core portfolio and is the only correct beta portfolio for a pension with a liability objective. The liability beta portfolio is the proper form of ALM or LDI. To create and maintain such a portfolio, a custom liability index is also required.

Several other prominent authors, especially Waring, have promoted the concept of "economic" value versus accounting and actuarial valuations. Waring (2004a, 2004b) produced two integrated papers titled "Liability-Relative Investing," which focus on an "economic" view of the liability and which break the return on the liability into beta and alpha components. This approach gives us a measure of the liability that is more relevant to the asset allocation problem than that provided by standard approaches.

Waring and Siegel produced a detailed account of why saving defined benefit pension plans is a good idea in their 2007 paper "Don't Kill the Golden Goose! Saving Pension Plans." They conclude that the first element needed to manage a defined benefit plan is an "economic" view of the liability. The only risks that can be hedged through investment policy and strategy are those that are correlated with market returns of one kind or another. Accounting values are not hedgeable because they are smoothed. Waring and Siegel recommend that corporations align at least some of their pension assets with liabilities and add one or more layers of additional return on top of that. The additional return can come from investing in risky assets, or it can come from skill at beating one or more markets (true alpha). In the face of a trend toward freezing defined benefit plans in favor of defined contribution plans, the authors provide four reasons why defined benefit plans are more cost effective and efficient than defined contribution plans.

In 2009, Waring and Whitney presented "An Asset–Liability Version of the Capital Asset Pricing Model with a Multi-Period Two-Fund Theorem," which introduced a new CAPM that incorporates "economic liabilities" and thus reveals a new risk-free asset: the liability-matching asset portfolio.

Westerheide and DeMairo (2008) made the point, in their article "Liability-Driven Investing," that in the wake of equity market gyrations and changes in pension accounting and funding rules, portfolio strategists have energetically been talking up LDI as an alternative framework for defining investment success for pension plans.

Adler (2009) observed, in "The New Way to Crunch Your Numbers," that LDI has taken hold among large U.S. pension funds, about half of which now use or are considering this strategy.

In 2011, *aiCIO Magazine* produced a special LDI issue that provided a collection of insightful articles by prominent LDI experts. Vivian, in "Strategy + Tactics for the Investment Nerd in Us," listed 12 issues to be considered when instituting an LDI strategy, with number 7 being the LDI benchmark. In addition to a crisp, clean benchmark, the issues to be considered include how, when, and from whom the benchmark constructor gets liability information. Juagietis, Thomas, and Gannon's article "LDI Benchmarking: When Does Basis Risk Matter?" made the point that the calculation of U.S. corporate plan liabilities is typically based on the yields of high-quality corporate bonds. They demonstrated that credit exposure becomes progressively more important as allocations to fixed income increase.

Public pensions have the largest deficits and the lowest funded ratios, a result that may be attributable to the Governmental Accounting Standards

Board (GASB) accounting rules, which smooth assets over five years and price liabilities at the ROA rate. Since 1999, this accounting practice has overvalued assets by 10% to 20% and undervalued liabilities by 30% to 60% versus economic values (market values). In "The Public Pension Crisis" (Ryan 2011), I described how the ROA misled pension trustees and consultants into making inappropriate asset allocation, benefit, and contribution decisions. All of these decisions are linked together. My solution to the public pension crisis starts with liabilities. Until a custom liability index is installed as the proper benchmark, I argued, all asset allocation, budget, and contribution decisions are in jeopardy.

In conclusion—and I acknowledge that this is a minority position—the advice of Fischer Black (1980) seems to ring true: "My message is simple: Almost every corporate pension fund should be entirely in fixed dollar investments."

This qualifies for 0.5 CE credits, inclusive of 0.5 SER credits.

Bibliography

Adler, David. 2009. "The New Way to Crunch Your Numbers." *Barron's* (22 June):32–35.

> "LDI certainly has taken hold among large U.S. pension funds, about half of which now use it or are considering doing so. The big liabilities of these funds—future payments to retirees—resemble long-term bonds and are extremely dependent on interest rates. If interest rates fall, it's harder for a fund to earn the money needed to make the payments. Therefore, the heart of most LDI strategies used by pension funds is to try to take this interest-rate risk off the table, so that assets and liabilities move in lock step when interest rates change." (p. 32)

Black, Fischer. 1980. "The Tax Consequences of Long-Run Pension Policy." *Financial Analysts Journal*, vol. 36, no. 4 (July/August):21–28.

> "I believe that every tax-paying firm's defined benefit pension fund portfolio should be invested entirely in bonds (or insurance contracts). Although the firm's pension funds are legally distinct from the firm, there is a close tie between the performance of the pension fund investments and the firm's cash flows. Sooner or later, gains or losses in pension fund portfolios will mean changes in the firm's pension contributions. Shifting from stocks to bonds in the pension funds will increase the firm's debt capacity, because it will reduce the volatility of the firm's future cash flows. Shifting from stocks to bonds will give an indirect tax benefit equal to the firm's marginal tax rate times the interest on the bonds." (p. 21)

Brick, John R. 2012. "Asset-Liability Management: Theory, Practice, and the Role of Judgment." Cuna CFO Council white paper (January):3–6.

> "The purpose of this paper is to analyze the manner in which asset-liability management (ALM) is currently practiced by depository institutions. ALM is the process that deals with interest rate risk (IRR) management. Inaccurate IRR assessments have led some institutions to unknowingly assume too much risk and others to assume insufficient risk. Accordingly it is imperative that this risk be properly measured and assessed to allow institutions to not only fulfill their economic role but to survive as well. ALM is a forward-looking process involving the simultaneous management of assets and liabilities to measure, monitor and control the effects of changing interest rates on income, asset values, liquidity and regulatory capital. The primary objective of an ALM analysis is to provide an early warning of possible financial problems resulting from the effects of changing interest rates on the existing balance sheet and income performance." (pp. 3, 6)

Choie, Kenneth S. 1992. "Caveats in Immunization of Pension Liabilities." *Journal of Portfolio Management*, vol. 18, no. 2 (Winter):54–69.

> "Immunization requires that the value of assets and the present value of liabilities be the same, and that the interest rate sensitivity or duration of the assets be the same as that of the liabilities. The first issue in immunization is establishment of the appropriate discount rates to compute the present value and the duration of a liability schedule. The question of the appropriate discount rates for a given liability schedule has crucial ramifications for construction of an asset portfolio to immunize the liability stream." (p. 54)

Collie, Bob. 2012. "LDI's Journey toward Greater Customization." *aiCIO Magazine*, vol. 4, no. 4 (LDI Special Issue):6–11.

> "The basic initial steps of an LDI program are an increase in the portfolio's sensitivity to interest rates and a reduction in equity holdings. These steps are similar no matter who is taking them. However, as the LDI program becomes more advanced and the link between the asset portfolio and the liabilities becomes stronger, a point is reached at which a greater degree of customization becomes necessary." (p. 6)

Davis, Joshua, Scott Porter, and Karen Steffen. 2009. "Public Plans: Using Risk Profiles to Manage Funding Goals." Paper presented at the Society of Actuaries Public Pension Finance Symposium, Chicago (May).

> "This paper will present two alternative practices that could promote fuller recognition of a plan's investment risks and that take into account the long-term nature of the benefit promises of maturing retirement systems. The paper will comprise a brief discussion of why the current funding policy, which aims for a 100-percent funded ratio (AVA/AAL), does not adequately reflect underlying portfolio risks. Then the main thrust of this paper will be a discussion of the key factors in a plan's risk profile, followed by two possible alternative funding policies that are designed to align a plan's underlying portfolio risks with its liabilities and maturity." (p. 1)

Ehrentreich, Norman. 2009. "The Asset Return–Funding Cost Paradox: The Case for LDI." Ehrentreich LDI Consulting & Research.

> "Pension regulations of the 1980s have effectively removed incentives for corporate plan sponsors to overfund their pension plans. Now, equity based investing strategies sooner or later lead to large funding shortfalls, and the inability of most plan sponsors to close them immediately makes them persistent. Therefore, the most basic requirement for converting eventual higher asset returns into lower

funding costs, i.e., having average funding levels of 100% or more, is regularly violated by most pension plans." (p. 1)

Exley, C.J., S.J.B. Mehta, and A.D. Smith. 1997. "The Financial Theory of Defined Benefit Pension Schemes." *British Actuarial Journal*, vol. 3, no. 4 (October):835–966.

"Increasingly, modern business and investment management techniques are founded on approaches to measurement of profit and risk developed by financial economists. This paper begins by analysing corporate pension provision from the perspective of such financial theory. The paper then proposes a successful blueprint for this mark-to-market valuation discipline and considers whether and how it can be applied to pension schemes both in theory and practice. It is asserted that adoption of this market based approach appears now to be essential in many of the most critical areas of actuarial advice in the field of defined benefit corporate pension provision and that the principles can in addition be used to establish more efficient and transparent methodologies in areas which have traditionally relied on subjective and arbitrary methods." (p. 835)

Fabozzi, Frank. 2001. "Managing Funds Against Liabilities." In *Bond Portfolio Management*. 2nd ed. Hoboken, NJ: John Wiley & Sons:549–574.

"The objectives of this chapter are to: explain what an immunization strategy is; demonstrate that the key to immunization is in constructing a portfolio to match the duration of the investment horizon; explain the risks associated with immunizing a portfolio and how that risk can be measured; discuss the factors to consider in creating an immunized portfolio; explain what contingent immunization is. In this chapter we will explain strategies for managing bond portfolios to satisfy predetermined liabilities. The two strategies we will discuss are immunization and cash flow matching." (p. 549)

———. 2005a. "Dedicated Bond Portfolios." In *The Handbook of Fixed Income Securities*. 7th ed. New York: McGraw-Hill:1103–1117.

"The dedicated bond portfolio, as it is frequently called, is a strategy that matches monthly cash flows from a portfolio of bonds to a prespecified set of monthly cash requirements of liabilities. Cash matching or prefunding these liabilities leads to the elimination of interest-rate risk and the defeasance of the liability. Applications for the dedicated strategy include pension benefit funding, defeasance of debt service, municipal funding of construction takedown schedules, structured settlement funding, GIC matching and funding of other fixed insurance products." (p. 1103)

———. 2005b. "Bond Immunization: An Asset/Liability Optimization Strategy." In *The Handbook of Fixed Income Securities*. 7th ed. New York: McGraw-Hill:1091–1101.

"Bond immunization is an important risk-control strategy used by the pension fund, insurance, banking, and thrift industries. In today's volatile markets, it is imperative that all asset/liability gaps be intentional. Immunization provides the tools to measure the interest-rate risk position an institution or a fund is taking with respect to its liabilities; it also provides the tools to minimize that risk when a minimum gap is desired." (p. 1091)

Fabozzi, Frank, and Ronald Ryan. 2005. "Reforming Pension Reform." *Institutional Investor* (January):84–88.

"Until pension liabilities are priced at the market, pension funds run the risk of an asset-liability disconnect. Liabilities should be priced off of a market yield curve. An ironclad pension accounting rule should be: If you cannot buy it, you cannot use it as a discount rate. Start with the Treasury zero-coupon yield curve. Use this yield curve to build custom liability indexes for each plan. Once a plan sponsor creates a custom index as a benchmark for liabilities, it can properly manage assets. Asset allocation and performance measurement models will be able to compare the growth and risk behavior of assets and liabilities by term structure. If assets are not measured against liabilities, they are likely to have the wrong index objective." (p. 88)

———. 2011. "Liability Index Fund: The Liability Beta Portfolio." *Journal of Financial Transformation*, vol. 33 (December):29–33.

"For corporate defined benefit plans, only a CLI [custom liability index] is the appropriate asset benchmark for liability-driven objectives. With a CLI, Beta and Alpha portfolios are redefined and can work in harmony with the true objective. The asset management guidelines of a pension plan can then take into account the risk/reward behavior of the true economic objective in establishing investment policy, especially the liability Beta portfolio which should be installed as the core portfolio." (p. 33)

"By definition, an index fund is the correct Beta portfolio that matches the index benchmark with such accuracy that the tracking error is nil with the Beta calculation at 1.00 and the correlation at or near 100. With a liability-driven objective, only a liability index fund could qualify as the Beta or matching portfolio. A liability index fund, by definition, requires an index that reflects a pension fund's liability term structure. Since each liability structure is unique, this calls for the creation of a custom liability index (CLI). Until the asset portfolio's cash flows match each monthly liability payment (i.e., liability term structure), the interest rate risk (systematic risk) that dominates the risk/reward behavior of pension liabilities cannot be hedged." (p. 31)

Financial Accounting Standards Board. 1985. "Statement of Financial Accounting Standards No. 87: Employers' Accounting for Pensions." FASB (December).

"Interest rates vary depending on the duration of investments; for example, U.S. Treasury bills, 7-year bonds, and 30-year bonds have different interest rates. . . . The disclosures required by this Statement regarding components of the pension benefit obligation will be more representationally faithful if individual discount rates to various benefit deferral periods are selected." (paragraph 199)

"In making those estimates, employers may also look to rates of return on high-quality fixed-income investments currently available and expected to be available during the period to maturity of the pension benefits." (paragraph 44)

———. 2006. "Statement of Financial Accounting Standards No. 158: Employers' Accounting for Defined Benefit Pension and Other Postretirement Plans." FASB (September).

"The objective of selecting assumed discount rates is to measure the single amount that, if invested at the measurement date in a portfolio of high-quality debt instruments, would provide the necessary future cash flows to pay the accumulated benefits when due. Notionally, that single amount, the accumulated post-retirement benefit obligation, would equal the current market value of a portfolio of high-quality zero-coupon bonds whose maturity dates and amounts would be the same as the timing and amount of the expected future benefit payments." (paragraph 144a)

Fisher, Lawrence, and Roman Weil. 1971. "Coping with the Risk of Interest-Rate Fluctuations: Returns to Bondholders from Naïve and Optimal Strategies." *Journal of Business*, vol. 44, no. 4 (October):408–431.

"A portfolio of investments is *immunized* for a holding period if its value at the end of the holding period, regardless of the course of interest rates during the holding period, must be at least as large as it would have been had the interest-rate function been constant throughout the holding period. If the realized return on the investment in bonds is sure to be at least as large as the appropriately computed yield to the horizon, then that investment is immunized." (p. 415)

Fong, H. Gifford, and Oldrich Vasicek. 1984. "A Risk Minimizing Strategy for Portfolio Immunization." *Journal of Finance*, vol. 39, no. 5 (December):1541–1546.

"Consider a fixed-income portfolio whose duration is equal to the length of a given investment horizon. It is shown that there is a lower limit on the change in the end-of-horizon value of the portfolio resulting from any given change in the structure of interest rates. This lower limit is the product of two terms, of which one is a function of the interest rate change only, and the other depends on the structure of the portfolio. Consequently, this second term provides a measure of immunization risk. If this measure is minimized, the exposure of the portfolio to any interest rate change is the lowest." (p. 1541)

Fooladi, Iraj J. 2000. "Risk Management with Duration Analysis." *Managerial Finance*, vol. 26, no. 3:18–28.

"This paper surveys current applications of duration analysis in risk management. Duration hedging or immunization draws on a second key mathematical property. By maintaining portfolio duration equal to the amount of time remaining in a planning horizon, the investment manager can immunize locking in the original promised return on the portfolio. Note that immunization seeks to tie the promised return, not to beat it. Because it requires no view of future interest rates, immunization is a passive strategy which may be particularly attractive when interest rates are volatile." (p. 20)

International Association of Insurance Supervisors. 2006. "Standard on Asset-Liability Management." IAIS Standard No. 13 (October):3–6.

"This paper describes best practices for asset-liability management (ALM) that a well managed insurer would be expected to follow and identifies 11 minimum requirements. Asset-liability management (ALM) is the practice of managing a business so that decisions and actions taken with respect to assets and liabilities are coordinated. The objective of ALM is not to eliminate risk. Rather, it is to manage risks within a framework that includes self-imposed limits. The IAIS requires that insurers have in place effective procedures for monitoring and managing their asset-liability positions to ensure that their assets and investment activities are appropriate to their liability and risk profiles and their solvency positions." (pp. 3, 5, 6)

Juagietis, Martin, Michael Thomas, and James Gannon. 2011. "LDI Benchmarking: When Does Basis Risk Matter?" *aiCIO Magazine,* vol. 3, no. 2 (LDI Special Issue):71–75.

"The calculation of U.S. corporate pension plan liabilities is typically based on the yields of high-quality corporate bonds. As plan sponsors ramp up their liability-driven investment (LDI) programs, at what point do the components of the liability-hedging portfolio begin to matter? This paper demonstrates that credit exposure becomes progressively more important as allocations to fixed income increase. We find that credit-like securities should comprise the majority of an LDI portfolio's liability-hedging exposure when the allocation to fixed income reaches around 60% of total portfolio assets, and that plan sponsors should seek higher-quality corporate bond exposures similar to those used in liability calculations when the percentage of fixed income assets increases beyond that." (p. 71)

Keintz, Richard J., and Clyde P. Stickney. 1980. "Immunization of Pension Funds and Sensitivity to Actuarial Assumptions." *Journal of Risk and Insurance*, vol. 47, no. 2 (June):223–239.

"Changes in market rates of return affect both the assets and liabilities of a pension fund. If these assets and liabilities are in a proper relationship with each other, however, the pension fund can be immunized from the change in market rates of return. The cornerstone of the immunization strategy is management of the duration, or weighted average life, of the asset portfolio. This paper discusses some of the factors to be considered in immunizing a medium-sized pension fund, including whether immunization is in fact a desirable strategy." (p. 223)

Koopmans, Tjalling C. 1942. "The Risk of Interest Fluctuations in Life Insurance Companies." Philadelphia: Penn Mutual Life Insurance.

"This paper develops the theory of the measurement of interest rate risks from its foundations, beginning with the question of which asset values (market or book) are economically relevant and therefore at risk. Upon this foundation, the paper builds a flexible and general theory of the measurement of interest rate risk that includes the familiar Macaulay-Redington theory of immunization as one special case." (p. 1)

Leibowitz, Martin L. 1986a. "The Dedicated Bond Portfolio in Pension Funds—Part I: Motivations and Basics." *Financial Analysts Journal*, vol. 42, no. 1 (January/February):68–75.

"Dedicated bond portfolios allow a corporate pension fund to take advantage of favorable fixed income markets and the actuarial system's willingness to provide special benefits for a minimum-risk investment approach. Purely as an investment approach, a dedicated portfolio serves as a least-risk asset, minimizing the risks involved in fulfilling a large class of nominal-dollar liabilities. Because the process is largely assumption-free, it provides the sponsoring corporation with an actuarially acceptable way to take advantage of available market interest rates to improve funding status." (p. 68)

———. 1986b. "The Dedicated Bond Portfolio in Pension Funds—Part II: Immunization, Horizon Matching and Contingent Procedures." *Financial Analysts Journal*, vol. 42, no. 2 (March/April):47–57.

"Immunization, horizon matching and various contingent schemes offer pension plan sponsors and managers an opportunity to minimize risk while retaining some degree of management discretion to pursue lower costs or higher returns. Immunization calls for the creation of a portfolio of bonds whose value coincides with the present value of a given schedule of liabilities and whose duration, or interest rate sensitivity, is the same as that of the liabilities. By specifying a minimum portfolio return somewhat below the available market rate, the manager can create a "cushion spread" that provides the basis for several contingent schemes. As long as the portfolio retains assets sufficient to meet the target return, it may be actively managed. When adverse market moves threaten this return, the portfolio must be converted into a dedicated mode that will assure the target return." (p. 47)

———. 1992. *Investing: The Collected Works of Martin L. Leibowitz*. Edited by Frank J. Fabozzi. Chicago: Probus Publishing.

"As director of Research at Salomon Brothers, Martin Leibowitz authored over 100 articles on a wide variety of investment topics. Fifty-seven of these papers have been chosen for this volume, some for their historical interest, but most for their continuing validity and current reference." (p. xi)

Leibowitz, Martin L., and Alfred Weinberger. 1982. "Contingent Immunization—Part I: Risk Control Procedures." *Financial Analysts Journal*, vol. 38, no. 6 (November/December):17–31.

"Central to the implementation of Contingent Immunization is an effective system for monitoring and risk control. This article details a number of the ideas and the potential problems involved in the development of risk control for Contingent Immunization. Part I, in this issue, reviews the basic concept of Contingent Immunization, showing how it fits within a framework encompassing both active management and immunization techniques, and outlines the main ingredients of a risk control process." (p. 17)

Macaulay, Frederick R. 1938. *Some Theoretical Problems Suggested by the Movement of Interest Rates, Bond Yields and Stock Prices in the United States since 1856*. New York: National Bureau of Economic Research.

"The time to maturity is not an accurate or even a good measure of 'duration.' 'Duration' is a reality of which 'maturity' is only one factor. Whether one bond represents an essentially shorter or an essentially longer term loan than another bond depends not only upon the respective 'maturities' of the two bonds but also upon their respective 'coupon rates' and under certain circumstances, on their respective 'yields.' Only if maturities, coupon rates and yields are identical can we say, without calculations, that the 'durations' of two bonds are the same. The duration of a stream of payments may be thought of as the average life of the stream." (p. 45)

Maloney, Kevin J., and Jess B. Yawitz. 1986. "Interest Rate Risk, Immunization and Duration." *Journal of Portfolio Management*, vol. 12, no. 3 (Spring):41–48.

> "The purpose of this paper is to develop a general model designed to specify how interest rate risk is related to the investor's holding period and to the particular stochastic process assumed to generate yield curve shifts. While each of these individual questions has been studied extensively, the literature has devoted relatively little attention to the development of a unifying model. In positioning this paper in the existing literature, our purpose has been to consolidate and extend the recent research that has addressed the question of interest rate risk in fixed income securities." (p. 41)

McDaniel, Kip. 2011. "LDI's Founding Document." *aiCIO Magazine,* vol. 3, no. 2 (LDI Special Issue):8–9.

> "The history of a formal LDI theory is littered, it seems, with false starts. Our conclusion is that, although historically a distinction has been drawn between asset and liability management by banks and pension funds, financial theory offers no good reason for this distinction. Time to stop treating pensions as anything special. They're the same as any other liability—and time to show that on the balance sheet." (pp. 8, 9)

Oracle Financial Services. 2008. "Asset Liability Management: An Overview." Oracle White Papers (www.oracle.com/us/industries/financial-services/045581.pdf).

> "Asset Liability Management (ALM) can be defined as a mechanism to address the risk faced by a bank due to a mismatch between assets and liabilities either due to liquidity or changes in interest rates. Apart from liquidity, a bank may also have a mismatch due to changes in interest rates as banks typically tend to borrow short term (fixed or floating) and lend long term (fixed or floating). The function of ALM is not just protection from risk. The safety achieved through ALM also opens up opportunities for enhancing net worth." (p. 2)

Ransenberg, Dan, and Jonathan Hobbs. 2011. "Overcoming Credit Downgrades: Four Ways to Improve Your Liability Hedge." *Investment Insights,* vol. 14, no. 2 (April).

> "In recent years, many US plan sponsors have adopted liability-driven investing (LDI) in response to changes in accounting standards (FASB 87) and funding requirements (Pension Protection Act). Others have embraced LDI after experiencing the devastating effects from leaving their liabilities unhedged over the past 10 years. Whatever the motivation, this change in strategy should significantly mitigate current pension plan volatility that is negatively impacting companies' balance sheets, income statements and cash flows." (p. 2)

Redington, F.M. 1952. "Review of the Principles of Life-Office Valuations." *Journal of the Institute of Actuaries*, vol. 78:286–340.

> "The word 'matching' implies the distribution of assets to make them, as far as possible, equally as vulnerable as the liabilities to those influences which affect both. The word 'matching' has such a wide and general connotation that it is necessary to adopt a new label with a more precise significance. For this purpose I use the word 'immunization' to signify the investment of the assets in such a way that the existing business is immune to a general change in the rate of interest." (p. 288)

Ryan, Ronald. 2003. "Testimony before the ERISA Advisory Council on Employee Welfare and Pension Benefit Plans." U.S. Department of Labor (July):1–23. As part of the "Report of the Working Group on Defined Benefit Plan Funding and Discount Rate Issues," produced by the Advisory Council on Employee Welfare and Pension Benefit Plans, dated 7 November 2003.

> "Liabilities should be priced at the market as a yield curve. A rule should be created, or enforced, that reads: If you cannot buy it, you cannot use it as a discount rate! Bond indexes are market-weighted; they're not liability weighted. Until a custom liability index is built for each pension plan, based upon the unique actuarial term structure of that plan, and priced off of real zero-coupon bonds, pensions are in jeopardy of managing to the wrong objective." (p. 9)

———. 2011. "The Public Pension Crisis." *IMCA Investments and Wealth Monitor* (July/August):18–20, 30.

> "The solution to the public pension and budget crisis starts with liabilities. Until a custom liability index (CLI) is installed as the proper benchmark, all asset allocation, asset management, benefit and contribution decisions will be based upon erroneous and misleading calculations. The benchmark must be a CLI because no two pensions are alike due to different salaries, mortality and plan amendments." (p. 30)

Samuelson, Paul. 1945. "The Effect of Interest Rate Increases on the Banking System." *American Economic Review*, vol. 35, no. 1 (March):16–27.

> "Current American discussions suggest that it may be advisable to assert the following propositions: (1) The banking system as a whole is not really hurt by an increase in the whole complex of interest rates. It is left tremendously better off by such a change. (2) A typical single bank, taken by itself, is not really hurt by an increase in the whole complex of interest rates. It is left better off by such a change. The author wishes to emphasize that he does not believe interest rate increases to be probable or desirable." (p. 16)

Seburn, Patrick W. 1991. "Evolution of Employer-Provided Defined Benefit Plans." *Monthly Labor Review* (December)16–23.

"The first pension plan seems to have begun in 1875 with the American Express Company. This newly created benefit was an incentive to get workers to come to the west to work for long periods of time. In order to qualify, retired workers had to have a minimimum of 20 years employment, were older than 60 years of age and were disabled. By 1986, the American Express pension plan had evolved into an extensive program covering more than 23,000 employees." (pp. 1-2)

Society of Actuaries. 2004. "Principles Underlying Asset Liability Management." SOA Exposure Draft (October).

"Asset Liability Management is the ongoing process of formulating, implementing, monitoring, and revising strategies related to assets and liabilities to achieve financial objectives, for a given set of risk tolerances and constraints. A consistent ALM structure can only be achieved for economic objectives. Various accounting measures are affected by rules that change the emergence of income and the reported book value of assets and liabilities. These measures can sometimes distort economic reality and produce results inconsistent with economic value. Because ALM is concerned with the future asset and liability cash flows, the natural focus of ALM is economic value. Entities that focus on economic value tend to achieve their financial objectives more consistently in the long term." (p. 6)

Thompson, Frank A. 1981. "Immunization of Pension Funds and Sensitivity to Actuarial Assumptions: Comment." *Journal of Risk and Insurance*, vol. 48, no. 1 (March):148–153.

"Some pension plans may desire to invest in corporate bonds where call features could alter maturity structure unexpectedly. A call provision allows the borrower to redeem bonds before maturity and thus may impose uncertainty on the length of the asset holding period." (p. 148)

U.S. Congress. 2006. "Pension Protection Act of 2006." Pub. L. 109–280, 120 Stat. 780 (www.gpo.gov/fdsys/pkg/PLAW-109publ280/pdf/PLAW-109publ280.pdf).

This legislation requires companies that have underfunded pension plans to pay higher premiums to the PBGC. The PPA significantly alters the rules for measuring plan assets and liabilities. Under the PPA, asset values may be smoothed over only two years and cannot vary from the market value by more than 10%. The PPA mandates use of a discount rate to determine the present value of benefit liabilities that is based on the two-year average of yield curves for high-quality corporate bonds. Specifically, there will be a separate discount rate for each of three segments: (1) within five years, (2) 6–20 years, and (3) more than 20 years.

Vanderhoof, I.T. 1972. "The Effects of Interest Rate Assumption and the Maturity Structure of the Assets of a Life Insurance Company." *Transactions of the Society of Actuaries*, vol. 24, no. 69AB (May and June):157–192.

"In this paper I shall: (1) argue that the interest rate assumption should concern itself with the long-term rate at which funds can be invested in the future; (2) demonstrate that, once such an assumption has been made about the investment environment, the crucial factor becomes the kind of investment the company has actually made—most particularly, the maturity pattern of the investments; (3) present the theory of immunization of investments to changes in interest rates and provide an extensive series of examples and formulas used in its implementation." (p. 157)

Vivian, Jay. 2011. "Strategy + Tactics for the Investment Nerd in Us." *aiCIO Magazine*, vol. 3, no. 2 (LDI Special Issue):16–17.

"By now the basics of pension liability-driven investing (LDI) are pretty well understood: There's downside risk because assets might go down, but even more if liability discount rates go down. The basics are things like really understanding how your liabilities will worsen if rates go down and alternative ways to hedge. But LDI is not a free lunch, you can lose a ton of money on it, and as they say, it has a lot of hair on it. Here are a dozen not-so-basic considerations that really should be thought through if you want to do LDI right." (p. 16)

Waring, M. Barton. 2004a. "Liability-Relative Investing." *Journal of Portfolio Management*, vol. 30, no. 4 (Summer):8–20.

"The notion of duration-matching, well-developed in the 1980s in nominal terms, is here extended to the dual durations of price sensitivity to real interest rates and to inflation rates. All assets (and liabilities) can be characterized more accurately using two durations instead of one." (p. 8)

———. 2004b. "Liability-Relative Investing II." *Journal of Portfolio Management*, vol. 31, no. 1 (Fall):40–53.

"This paper revisits and updates the technology for calculating surplus efficient frontiers and surplus asset allocation, to separately incorporate both systematic and unsystematic, or beta and alpha, characteristics. We develop and incorporate an economic view of the liability, also in beta and alpha terms. This gives us a measure of the liability that is more relevant to the asset allocation problem than provided by standard approaches." (p. 40)

Waring, M. Barton, and Laurence B. Siegel. 2007. "Don't Kill the Golden Goose! Saving Pension Plans." *Financial Analysts Journal*, vol. 63, no. 1 (January/February):31–45.

> "The first element of 'new' technology needed to manage DB plan risk and cost is an *economic* view of the liability. The only risks that are helpful to know about are the risks that can be hedged through investing the assets. Such risks are those in the liability that are market related—that is, correlated with the returns of assets or indices available in the markets. Therefore, sponsors need to set aside the actuarial and accounting views of the liability and rediscount the cash flows at appropriate, market-related rates. Plus, they need to understand how these market-related values, economically sensible measures of periodic pension cost, and economically required contributions change as market interest rates change." (p. 36)

Waring, Barton, and Duane Whitney. 2009. "An Asset–Liability Version of the Capital Asset Pricing Model with a Multi-Period Two-Fund Theorem." *Journal of Portfolio Management*, vol. 35, no. 4 (Summer):111–130.

> "The authors present a new capital asset pricing model (CAPM) that incorporates investors' deferred spending plans, or 'economic liabilities'—the underlying purpose behind all investments—and thus reveal a new risk-free asset, the investor's liability-matching asset portfolio." (p. 111)

Westerheide, Daniel, and John DeMairo. 2008. "Liability-Driven Investing." *Financial Executive* (January/February).

> "Pension plan sponsors have traditionally invested, with varying degrees of success, by navigating the tradeoff between investment risk and reward by seeking maximum returns within acceptable volatility parameters. Now, however, prompted by equity market gyrations and changes in pension accounting and funding rules in recent years, portfolio strategists have been energetically talking up an alternative framework for defining investment 'success' for pension plans: liability-driven investing (LDI)." (p. 1)

Williams, Eliot. 1992. "Managing Asset/Liability Portfolios—An Overview." *AIMR Conference Proceedings* (June):1–5.

> "New ideas have developed during the past few years in the understanding and practice of asset/liability management. Although many of these ideas surfaced in response to the challenges and difficulties many financial institutions faced in the 1980s, they also extend the underlying precepts of modern portfolio theory into new areas of application and make use of some new tools for risk management." (p. 1)

Made in the USA
Monee, IL
04 November 2026

67382302R00015